# THE SUNDERLAND
# FLYING=BOAT
# ~QUEEN~
## VOLUME I

*John Evans.*

## JOHN EVANS

4

# FOREWORD

Flight Lieutenant L.H. Baveystock, DSO, DFC, DFM
a photograph taken in late 1944.

My first sight of a Sunderland flying-boat was from the deck of a crowded troopship in the North Atlantic in September, 1941. Part of a large slow convoy, we were nine days out from Halifax with still five more perilous days yet to pass before reaching England. I was one of several hundred fledgling airmen returning after training in Canada. The Sunderland's arrival at dawn soon had the ships' rails jammed with men, all thrilled at the sight of this beautiful aircraft under whose protective screen we now sailed. Loud were the expressions of both praise and gratitude to its captain and crew who had flown so far from their base to find us in this limitless ocean. Like many of my comrades I wondered how it would feel to fly such a superb aircraft and to be entrusted with the lives of innumberable ships and men on whom Britain depended for its very existence.

But I was not to find out until October, 1942, when, after a short spell of operational flying in Bomber Command, I was posted to 461 Squadron flying Sunderlands from Poole Harbour. There, as a second pilot, I discovered the close bond which existed among Sunderland crews, and the affection in which they held their aircraft. For in the air it was completely viceless and could be thrown around like a giant Tiger Moth. Its sheer size with its galley and ward room enabled crews to move around freely and swap duties thus keeping fresh and vigilant during long flights of up to sixteen hours.

In June, 1943, I joined 201 Squadron as a skipper, flying Atlantic patrols from Castle Archdale on Lough Erne. It now became my task to give protection to the Atlantic convoys.

Two months before D-Day 201 Squadron uplifted to Pembroke Dock to play its part in protecting the supporting ships of the invasion fleet. Now equipped with the Frazer Nash twin gun front turret plus four fixed pilot's guns the Sunderland had become a most formidable aircraft. And with the fitting of Mark III radar and multiple flare dropping equipment it was able to find and attack surfaced U-Boats by night and day. The work carried out by its crews was of tremendous value in the final liberation of Europe.

When I flew my last flight in November, 1945, my pilot's log book revealed that in 1470 hours I made 311 flights in no less than 79 individual Sunderlands. And I never found a "bad un" among the lot. What better tribute can I pay to this unique flying-boat which truly earned the title of "Queen of the Skies".

My thanks and those of hundreds of other "Sunderlanders" are due not only to the designers but also to the huge workforce who built 749 of these splendid flying-boats.

*Les Baveystock*
*(Flight Lieutenant L.H. Baveystock DSO, DFC, DFM RAFVR)*

*Auckland, New Zealand, June 1987.*

# INTRODUCTION

The Sunderland ranks among the truely great aircraft of all time. It stands alongside the Spitfire, Hurricane, Lancaster and Mosquito - all great British designs. Even to the layman the name Sunderland conjures up visions of flying-boats and an aviation era which sadly is no longer.

Conceived in the early Thirties, the Sunderland was still in military use in the Sixties, and today a handful remain as reminders of a glorious chapter in aviation history.

The Sunderland was a product of the Short Brothers Company whose flying-boat and seaplane designs led the world. Its pedigree was impeccable, spanning the decades through types such as the Cromarty, Singapore I, II and III, Calcutta, Rangoon, Kent and Sarafand.

Born out of Air Ministry Specification R/33 of November, 1933 - which called for a long-range general purpose flying-boat with four engines - the S25 Sunderland first flew at Rochester four years later. At the controls was John Lankester Parker, the renowned Chief Test Pilot of Short Brothers.

That first flight - by K4774 on 16th October, 1937 - began a legend which today, 50 years on, is undiminished by the passage of time. By its performance, its reliability, its strength, its deeds, the Sunderland earned itself the great respect of those who flew and serviced it, and the undying affection of a whole host of others to whom the name Sunderland meant much more than just another aircraft type.

The Sunderland's RAF service career totalled 21 years - a record then unsurpassed by any other type. It flew in every theatre of war being called upon to undertake tasks far removed from its original role of 'general reconnaissance'. In the Mediterranean it played a vital part in the evacuations of Greece and Crete; in the Far East it flew supplies behind the Japanese lines to Chindit forces; in the Atlantic it made several daring air-sea rescues of survivors of ships or aircraft.

As a submarine hunter the Sunderland earned its spurs in the bitter war fought around the Atlantic convoy lifeline and in the 'the Bay' - the U-Boat's transit area across the Bay of Biscay. The attrition rate was high on both sides.

As a doughty fighter the Sunderland won the grudging respect of its Luftwaffe opponents in some remarkable air-to-air battles, a classic clash in May, 1943, resulting in one Australian Sunderland repelling the determined attacks of no less than eight Junkers Ju88 fighters. The Luftwaffe called the Sunderland Fliegende Stachelschwein - the Flying Porcupine - a title earned the hard way.

To men of many nations the Sunderland was more than just a machine - it was house and home, a self-contained unit able to operate for prolonged periods away from home base.

In wartime, 20 squadrons flew Sunderlands operationally - several of the squadrons being manned by crews from the Empire. Frenchmen and Norwegians also had their own squadrons of Sunderlands operating under the control of the RAF.

In peacetime the Sunderland was to soldier on for another 14 years in RAF service and was not finally retired from a military role until withdrawn by the Royal New Zealand Air Force in 1967.

The last of 749 Sunderlands built - SZ599 - was launched at Short and Harland's, Belfast, on 14th June, 1946. Production had been centred on four locations - Shorts at Rochester; Short and Harland at Belfast; Blackburns at Dumbarton, and a second Shorts factory in the beautiful surroundings of Lake Windermere.

Post-war the Sunderland users included the RAF, Royal New Zealand Air Force, South African Air Force and the French Navy. It is thanks to the longevity of the Sunderland, and its late service with New Zealand and France, that today a few of this most famous of all the flying-boats remain for future generations to see.

This book is not intended to be a history of the Short Sunderland but is merely a reflection in photographs of some of the many and varied roles this great flying-boat was called upon to perform in war and peace over a lengthy period of history.

It is meant, in this 50th Anniversary year of the Sunderland's first flight, to be a small tribute to a great aircraft and to the people who flew, serviced and supported it.

Hopefully it will also serve as a reminder of the splendid part flying-boats have played in our aviation history.

The emphasis of this book is perceptibly towards the former RAF Station at Pembroke Dock. This is intentional, reflecting not only the Author's particular interest in the fine history of Pembroke Dock but also the major contribution this station made to the military story of the Sunderland.

Pembroke Dock was home to Sunderland squadrons for 19 years and the station became - in the mid-war years - the largest operational flying-boat base in the world. RAF Pembroke Dock's history is indelibly linked with that of the Sunderland - each contributed immeasurably to the success of the other.

# I. LINEAGE

**Trimotor...**The Short Rangoon served with two RAF Squadrons between 1931 and 1936. Distinctive with its three uncowled Jupiter IXF engines, it was derived from the civil Calcutta flying-boat. Just six Ragoons were built for the RAF, serving first with 203 Squadron at Basra and then with 210 Squadron at Pembroke Dock. Armed with single Lewis guns in the nose and the two waist gun positions, the Rangoon could carry up to 1,000 lb of bombs on underwing racks. S1433, seen here when with 203 Squadron, was the first Rangoon and first flew on 24th September, 1930. It was also the last in service performing an unsung but necessary role as a crew trainer for Imperial Airways from 1936-1938, using the civilian registration G-AEIM. It was subsequently scrapped.                 *H. MARSHALL*

**Biplane...**A fine study of Singapore III K8568. The last of Short Brothers' splendid line of military biplane flying-boats, the Singapore III served the RAF well between 1935 and 1941, and soldiered on with the New Zealand Air Force until 1945. Powered by four Rolls Royce Kestrels in tandem pairs, the Mark III had a top speed of 145 mph and a range of 1,000 miles. Thirty-seven Mark IIIs were built for the RAF, the last being delivered in June, 1937. K8568 did not survive to see war service. It was delivered to 210 Squadron at Pembroke Dock early in 1937 and was Struck Off Charge following an accident in May, 1939, when with 204 Squadron. *MRS. J. BUTCHER*

**Civil sister...**Equally famous with the Sunderland was its civil stablemate, the S23 C-Class flying-boat. G-ADHL, Canopus, was the first of a long line of 'Empires' and first flew on 3rd July, 1936 - 15 months before the prototype Sunderland. The C-Class boats - all given names beginning with C - wrote a whole chapter in British aviation history by opening up much of the Empire through regular air services. Canopus, first of 42 'Empires', survived the war only to be broken up in 1946 having logged 15,000 hours and flown over two million miles. Four of the Empire Class were impressed into RAF service, two being lost during the Norwegian Campaign in May, 1940. The others served with 119 Squadron at Bowmore and one (AX659, formerly Clio) crashed in August, 1941.                                  *AVIATION PHOTO NEWS*

**In wolf's clothing...**One of the three Short 'G' Class flying-boats, seen in RAF colours. First flown nine months after the prototype Sunderland, the G-Boats were larger than either the Empires or the Sunderlands, having a wingspan of 134 ft. and a length of 101 ft. Powered by four 1,380 hp Bristol Hercules the G-Boats topped 209 mph and were intended as mail carriers across the Atlantic. The war changed these plans and the three 'boats' - G-AFCI Golden Hind, G-AFCJ Golden Fleece and G-AFCK Golden Horn - were 'called up' by the RAF. Given 'teeth' in the form of three Boulton-Paul Mark II turrets (two in dorsal positions and one in the tail) and ASV radar they joined 'G' Flight at Bowmore, Islay, early in 1941. 'G' Flight became 119 Squadron in March and two months later the G-Boats went to Mountbatten for special flights to Gibraltar and the Middle East. X8274 (formerly Golden Fleece) was lost on one such flight, on 20th June, 1941. When en route to Gibraltar engine trouble forced a ditching in heavy swell off Cape Finisterre. Only five of the 12 crew and two passengers survived, ironically to be rescued by a German U-Boat and to become PoWs. By the end of the year the surviving G-Boats had been returned to BOAC.                                  *REAL PHOTOGRAPH/MAP B60059*

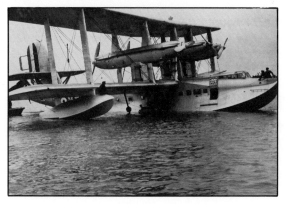

**One and only...**Just one example of the six-engined Short Sarafand was built and it was impressive by any standards. With a wing span of 120 ft. and a length of nearly 90 ft. it first flew at the hands of John Parker on 30th June, 1932, being at that time the world's second largest aircraft. The Sarafand - serial number S1589 - was powered by 825 hp Rolls Royce Buzzards in three tandem pairs. It spent much of its four-year career at MAEE Felixstowe, being the workhorse for a wide range of experimental flight tests. S1589 was in the public eye in June, 1935, when it headed a formation of prototype flying-boats to the RAF Display at Hendon. A year later it was scrapped at Felixstowe, outmoded by the new generation of monoplane flying-boats.

*RAF MUSEUM P14841*

# II. PROTOTYPE

H.1057 (a)

**First of the many...** The Sunderland prototype K4774 in various poses. K4774 emerged into the limelight from Shorts No 3 Shop at Rochester on 14th October, 1937. After successful taxiing trials the Sunderland first flew on 16th October with John Parker at the controls, Harold Piper as co-pilot and George Cotton as engineer. Two flights, totalling 45 minutes, were made on the first day followed by a 55 minute flight on the 21st and another of 1 1/4 hours duration on the 28th - the Sunderland had well and truly arrived. Originally flown with 950 hp Bristol Pegasus X engines and unswept wings, K4774 returned to No 3 Shop for installation of 1010 hp Pegasus XXII, modifications to the main step and for the wings to have a 4 1/2 degree sweep-back. Flight tests resumed on 7th March, 1938, and a month later the silver Sunderland was delivered to the Marine Aircraft Experimental Establishment at Felixstowe. It performed many useful experiments and trials during its wartime service, including tests which resulted in the faired main step on the Mark III. When at Helensburgh with the MAEE in 1942, K4774 was damaged when a depth charge exploded on impact. The prototype's eventual fate is not confirmed but it was obviously scrapped when its useful life was over.

Photographs show: K4774 taxiing, its graceful bulk much at home on the water. *SHORT BROTHERS H1057(a)*

The prototype airborne - a truly historic picture.
*SHORT BROTHERS H1058*

Power and perfection - a head-on view of the prototype.
*THE AEROPLANE VIA MRS D DEAKIN*

# III. SILVER WINGS

**Showing the flag...**Six silver Sunderlands, photographed from a seventh, in formation over the South Coast sometime in 1939.
*MRS NANCY OWEN*

**The bridge...**View into the cockpit of a Mark I Sunderland. The circular control wheel is hidden behind the skipper's seat on the left. *BILL SIMPSON*

**Record breaker...**The second production Sunderland, L2159, first flew on 4th May, 1938. Five days later it was delivered to MAEE Felixstowe to share trials with the prototype. Cleared for tropical service L2159 was the first Sunderland to go to the Far East, being flown by a crew from 210 Squadron, Pembroke Dock. Captained by Flight Lieutenant W A Hughes the aircraft left the UK on 9th June and its first flight leg, to Gibraltar, set the standard for the whole journey. L2159 flew the 1,250 miles in eight hours and the next day covered 1,200 miles to Malta in 6³/4 hours, averaging 177 mph. That same day another leg was flown to Alexandria. Other stops en route were Habbaniyah, Bahrein, Karachi, Gwalior, Calcutta, Rangoon and Mergui, arriving in record time at Seletar on 22nd June to be handed over to 230 Squadron. Hughes and his crew came home more sedately - flying a Singapore III. L2159's days ended dramatically back in the UK in May, 1941, when it was damaged beyond repair in an air raid on Greenock. *RAF MUSEUM P20034*

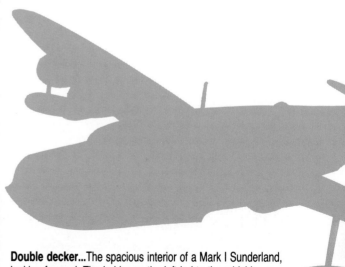

**Double decker...**The spacious interior of a Mark I Sunderland, looking forward. The ladder on the left led to the midships gun positions and, ultimately, to the flight deck. *MRS D DEAKIN*

**Seletar bound...**L2164 seen at Felixstowe soon after its first flight on 30th June, 1938. A week later, again with John Parker at the controls, this aircraft took several VIPs aloft. A 210 Squadron crew flew L2164 to Seletar where it became one of the eight Sunderlands of 230 Squadron - three of the aircraft being funded by a gift of £300,000 from the Federated Malay States' Sultans. L2164 later flew in the turmoil of the Mediterranean war and - still with 230 Squadron - became another statistic of the Battle for Malta when, on 10th March 1941, it was set on fire in an air raid and sank in St. Paul's Bay.                    *RAF MUSEUM P8830*

**Pre-war casualty...**One of the second production batch of Sunderlands, L5801, photographed over a tropical landscape. L5801 was the second Sunderland to be lost in RAF service, crashing on take-off in the Johore Straits on 5th June, 1939. It was one of 230 Squadron's aircraft.                    *RAF MUSEUM P16292*

**To the rescue...**L5802, RF, of 204 Squadron, one of the aircraft which rescued the crew of the SS *Kensington Court* in September, 1939. For this L5802's pilot, Flight Lieutenant John Barrett, won a DFC. L5802 had an eventful life, serving with 210, 204, 201, 95 and 461 RAF Squadrons. 'Pensioned off' into a training role with 4 OTU it crashed at Alness in a night landing on 16th January, 1943 and sank. In the months leading up to the beginning of the war 204 Squadron was one of the three RAF squadrons to re-equip with the Sunderland. Mountbatten was 204's home station.                    *JOHN POINTER*

**First Sunderlanders...**Officers and senior NCOs of 210 Squadron, Pembroke Dock in 1938. Standing (left to right): Flight Sergeant Johnson; Sergeant -----; Sergeant Pilot Jewiss; Pilot Officer Adams; Pilot Officer (later Group Captain) H D Newman; Pilot Officer Allan Ainslie; Sergeant Pilot (later Wing Commander) Chapman; Sergeant ----; Sergeant Pilot (later Flight Lieutenant) John Tee. Seated (left to right): Flying Officer W A Hughes; Flight Lieutenant Watts-Read; Squadron Leader (later Group Captain) Ashton; Wing Commander W N Plenderleith (Commanding Officer); Squadron Leader (later Air Commodore) W H Hutton; Flight Lieutenant (later Group Captain) Franklin; Pilot Officer Sinclair.                    *GROUP CAPTAIN H D NEWMAN*

**Men of PD...**The familiar Royal Naval Dockyard wall forms a solid backcloth as the officers and men of 228 Squadron line up for an official photograph early in 1939. The Squadron had reformed at Pembroke Dock in December, 1936, and two years later began exchanging its Stranraers for Sunderlands. *H BUXTON/MRS D DEAKIN*

**Crowd-puller...**Stars of the May, 1939, Empire Air Day at RAF Pembroke Dock were the Sunderlands of the resident 210 and 228 Squadrons. L5799, of 210 Squadron - wearing the Squadron's pre-war code letters VG - was open to the public, many of the 7,000 crowd taking advantage of this to look inside the silver giant. Within 12 months L5799 - by now with 204 Squadron - had become a war casualty. Sunderlands were pressed into reconnaissance duties during the ill-fated Norwegian Campaign and L5799 was lost off Norway on 7th April, 1940. *GROUP CAPTAIN G A BOLLAND*

**In the Med...**A 228 Squadron Sunderland on the Imperial Airways slipway at Alexandria in the summer of 1939. The front Frazer Nash FN11 turret, with its single gun, is shown to advantage. The airman on the left is well equipped to ward off the searing Mediterranean sun.
*EDGAR MORGAN*

**Variation on a theme...**N6135 at Kalafrana, Malta, in the summer of 1939. This 228 Squadron aircraft exhibits an unusual codes combination. In the months running up to the outbreak of war 228 Squadron used TO as its code letters and on N6135 the letters were split by the serial number. On 10th September, 1939, N6135 - by now wearing the codes BH-U - returned to the UK with the Squadron. When landing downriver from Pembroke Dock its floats were damaged and later, while under tow, N6135 turned turtle and sank. It was salvaged but was too badly damaged to repair.
*DON PURCELL*

**In fashion...**Eight airmen, sporting a variety of headgear to shield against the sun, line up on N9020/TO-W of 228 Squadron, somewhere in the Mediterranean, 1939. N9020 served only with 228 Squadron, being reported missing over the Ionian Sea on 1st November, 1940.
*G MORGAN*

# IV. ON WINGS OF WAR

**Press call...**Mediterranean veteran N9029, NM-V of 230 Squadron, photographed by *Daily Mail* war correspondent Alexander Clifford, January 1941. A long serving Mark I, N9029 was regarded as an exceptional aircraft by the crew which flew it for 18 months and more. In the cauldron of the Mediterranean war N9029 was in the forefront of the action, taking part in the Greek Campaign (during which the crew fitted a new tailplane) and operating from beleagured Malta, attached to 228 Squadron. Captain of V-Victor for over 18 months to mid-1941 was Flight Lieutenant Alan Lywood. He and his crew completed over 1,000 operational hours in N9029, more than any other aircraft in the Middle East at that time. During the whole operational tour the aircraft never failed to take off on any occasion but was once forced to land on the sea for the crew to repair a leaking hydraulic system. N9029's crew at the time was: Flight Lieutenant Lywood, Flying Officer D K Bednall, Pilot Officer A D Jillings and Sergeants Hughes, Smith, Waterland, Allen, McCran and Walker. While still on 230 Squadron strength, N9029 was lost in a crash on New Year's Day, 1943.                   *J L WATSON/RAF MUSEUM PO2790*

**Taking the strain...**Corporal Bill Butler and ACI Bill Odgers bombing up a 204 Squadron Sunderland at RAF Mountbatten c September 1939              *SQUADRON LEADER W F BUTLER*

**Aussie boat...**W3984, officially a Mark II but still retaining the midships gun positions housing single Vickers K-gun mountings. This aircraft gave sterling service with 10 Squadron, RAAF, for which it carries the well-known code combination RB. Built at Rochester as one of just 43 Sunderland Mark IIs, W3984 was Struck Off Charge in June, 1944.              *IMPERIAL WAR MUSEUM CH7502*

**Factory fresh...**Rochester built Mark III JM682 on its beaching gear at Pembroke Dock, probably prior to allocation to 204 Squadron. JM682 survived the war and was sold as scrap in February, 1947. *GROUP CAPTAIN A M CAREY*

**On patrol...**Mark II W3989, DQ-L of 228 Squadron on Atlantic anti-submarine patrol, Summer 1942. After its operational service divided between 202 and 228 Squadrons, W3989 went to 4 OTU and finally 302 Ferry Training Unit. When with the unit it was involved in an accident in October, 1944, running onto rocks at Castle Archdale. It was finally Struck Off Charge in February, 1945, its job well and truely done. *SQUADRON LEADER FRED JACKSON/RAF MUSEUM P15665*

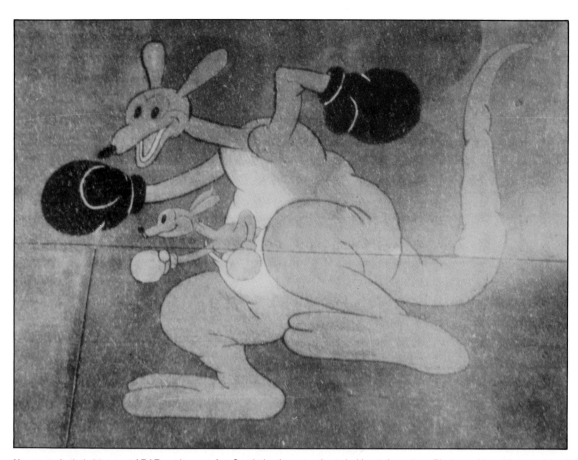

**Nose art...**In their 21 years of RAF service very few Sunderlands were adorned with art characters. Photographic evidence exists of these two examples, both on 228 Squadron aircraft. The boxing kangaroos mascot was painted on Mark III W4026, M-Mother, the ill-fated Sunderland of Flight Lieutenant Frank Goyen, RAAF. W4026 crashed in Caithness, north-east Scotland, on 25th August, 1942, killing Goyen and all but one of his crew together with the Duke of Kent, a passenger on the flight from Invergordon to Iceland. *JOE AYLING*

This airman figure was painted above the door of Mark III ML770, P-Peter. It was later removed by order of 228's then Squadron Commander, Wing Commander Pat Lombard. *BERNARD LYONS*

**African queen...**Sunderland Mark III K-King (possibly EJ163) of 95 Squadron seen in West African skies. Formed at Oban in January, 1941, out of a Flight of 210 Squadron, the new Squadron soon headed for warmer climes. First home station was Freetown, West Africa, and the Sunderlands' 'beat' was the South Atlantic, involving long, dull convoy escort and anti-submarine patrols. Later bases were Jui, Bathhurst and Port Etienne, the squadron finally disbanding at Bathurst in June, 1945.

*RAF MUSEUM P7946*

**Xmas fayre...** Greeting card from 230 Squadron which, at Christmas time, 1940, was heavily involved in the Mediterranean war. For this second Christmas of the conflict the Squadron was determined not to miss out on traditions, even though they were many miles from home. *Dumana* was an 8,427 gross ton liner owned by the British India Steam Navigation Company and used as an accommodation ship by RAF flying-boat personnel. Christmas, 1940, saw *Dumana* at Alexandria; three years later - on Christmas Eve, 1943 - the liner met her end. When on a voyage from Port Etienne to Takoradi, with an RAF contingent on board, *Dumana* was torpedoed and sank in a short time. Seven of the RAF and 24 of the crew lost their lives as the liner plunged to her last resting place off the Ivory Coast.

*HARRY THRELFALL*

**In Angle Bay...**ML770, wearing the Pembroke Dock station identification number 1 in place of code letters, on a 'trot' at Angle, 1944.

*BERNARD LYONS*

**Gunner's view...**Looking out over the four Brownings in the Frazer Nash FN13 tail turret of Mark I P9623, 'The Lazy E', of 210 Squadron. Usual occupant of this turret was Sergeant Sid Sait. P9623 was one of 95 Squadron's first aircraft in January, 1941. En route to West Africa P9623 was forced to land in Portuguese waters and aircraft and crew were interned. The crew was repatriated and the Sunderland was sold to the Portuguese.

*SID SAIT*

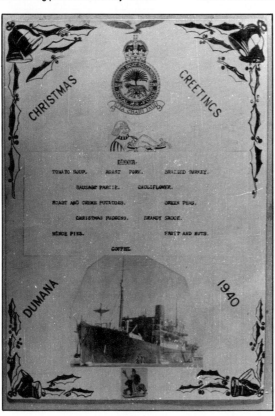

**Top turret...**W3990 awaits the call to action, January, 1942. This Rochester produced Mark II has a Botha-type FN7 twin gun dorsal turret, replacing the open Vickers K-gun mountings. It also has the impressive array of ASV Mark II radar aerials, giving the aircraft a 'stickleback' look. W3990 served with 228 and 202 Squadrons before going to 4 OTU at Alness. Here it sank during a gale on 15th February, 1943.
*SHORT BROS VIA MRS NANCY OWEN*

**Alongside...**Sunderland 2-F (probably ML774 of 461 Squadron, RAAF) receiving attention to its starboard beaching gear at Pembroke Dock, December, 1944. All this and much more was part of a day's work for the men of the Marine Craft Sections.
*DR DAVID STEWART*

**Out on a wing...**Canvas covers being removed from the Pegasus XVIII engines of a Sunderland at Pembroke Dock.
*DR DAVID STEWART*

**Moored up...**The DG code combination betrays the ownership of ML773 at Pembroke Dock. A Mark III of 422 Squadron, RCAF, it carries the individual identity letter of either P, B or R. ML773 went into storage post war, being Struck Off Charge in March, 1947.

*DR DAVID STEWART*

**Passing by...**T9072, a Mark I, taxiing past. It carries the markings KG-F of 204 Squadron, its first unit. While with 204 Squadron T9072 hit unchartered rocks at Reykjavik but was repaired. Transferred to 10 Squadron, RAAF, it was tragically lost on 5th December, 1941, when flying from Oban to Pembroke Dock to collect the new Commanding Officer. The port outer engine failed and T9072 crashed into the sea off Anglesey, North Wales. Four of the 15 on board were killed. *RAF MUSEUM P16924*

**Power on...**RN284, NS-C, of 201 Squadron at full power, c 1945. A Blackburn built Mark V, RN284 served in war and peace with 201 Squadron (also coded NS-G, A-F and 201-F) as well as 235 Operational Conversion Unit. After its RAF days it was transferred to the French Navy in December, 1957.

*MR AND MRS GEORGE LONSDALE*

**Farewell...**Sunderlands of 201 Squadron make a final flight down the Donegal Corridor as the Squadron prepares to leave its main wartime station, RAF Castle Archdale, August, 1945. The Corridor was the strip of neutral Irish Free State territory over which the RAF were permitted to fly in order to reach the Atlantic. This permission was granted in 1941 after delicate negotiations with the Irish Prime Minister, Eamonn De Valera. In this formation are NS-H, RN285, NS-G, RN284 and NS-O. RN285 first served with 228 Squadron and later with 4 OTU. It was Struck Off Charge in May, 1953. *RAF MUSEUM P17735*

**Alight Lough Erne...**Sunderland IIIA, YI-C, of 423 Squadron, RCAF, on the water at RAF Castle Archdale, Northern Ireland. The aircraft cannot be positively identified but was one of the last batch of Belfast built Sunderlands with Pegasus engines. The installation in these of 9 cm ASV VIc radar, with spilt scanners under the wingtips, led to the designation Mark IIIA. One of two Canadian Sunderland Squadrons, 423 formed at Oban in March, 1942, moving to Lough Erne in November. Here it remained until the war's end. The Squadron Motto was: 'We Search and Strike'. *RAF MUSEUM P17843*

**Vive La France...**French personnel pose with their Sunderlands at Pembroke Dock in the summer of 1943 before flying out to West Africa. In great security the French were trained on Sunderlands at PD, then took their new charges out to Dakar. *GROUP CAPTAIN A M CAREY*

**Best blues...**Officers and men of 461 Squadron, Royal Australian Air Force, line up for an official squadron photograph sometime in the late summer or early autumn of 1943. One of Pembroke Dock's camouflaged hangers forms the backdrop. There are 54 officers in front of the Sunderland with 64 men of the wings and engines; five in the nose well and one in the port door. The censor's hand has obliterated the ASV aerial array. Born out of the famous 10 Squadron, RAAF, in April, 1942, 461 was a worthy offspring. Flying first from RAF Mountbatten, 461 later moved to Hamworthy, Poole Harbour, and finally to PD in April, 1943. It was disbanded there in June, 1945, having written a fine chapter in the story of this station. *SQUADRON LEADER KEN FIELD*

**In focus...**A squadron group photographed in front of the Garrison Theatre, the former Royal Dockyard Church, at Pembroke Dock during the war years. It is believed that this is a 119 Squadron group, the squadron being stationed at Pembroke Dock for two periods prior to disbanding there in April, 1943. This squadron had a chequered flying-boat history. Forming with G-Class boats at Bowmore, Islay, in March, 1941, it flew a mixed bag of aircraft before converting fully onto Sunderlands. *F ALDERTON*

**Men of 228...**The Commanding Officer of 228 Squadron, Wing Commander Pat Lombard, posing with one of his successful U-Boat hunting crews, skippered by Flight Lieutenant George Bunting, DFC, at RAF Pembroke Dock, 1944. Back row (left to right): S Powell, V Drew, J H Lewis, P R Johnson, H Pridmore, W P Wood, J B Wells. Front row (left to right): J Court, G Bunting, Wing Commander Lombard, O T Brown, D Tylor.                                                                              *GEORGE BUNTING*

**Men of 201...**Wing Commander Guy Van der Kiste, DSO, Commanding Officer of 201 Squadron, with his senior pilots and staff at Pembroke Dock in early 1944. PD was 201's base over the D-Day period and the Squadron had considerable success during this time. Front row (left to right): Flight Lieutenant Wally Walters, Squadron Leader 'Babe' Ruth, Wing Commander Van der Kiste, Squadron Leader Powell, Flight Lieutenant Les Baveystock. Not all the others have been identified but they include the Intelligence Officer, Malcolm Anderson, the Medical Officer, Ivor Wiles, Ernie Norris and Harry Martin.                          *M N ANDERSON*

**Men of 461...** The crew of S-Sugar, 461 Squadron, RAAF, at Pembroke Dock, 1943. Front row (left to right): 'Junior' Weeks, Pilot Officer John Dobson, Flight Lieutenant Russ Baird (captain), Flying Officer Doug Hughes, Ross Watts, Johnnie Temple. Back row (left to right): Fred Salisbury, 'Jock' Stewart, Ron MacKellar, Ken 'Lofty' Field, Gerry 'Paddy' Watson, Terry Williams. It was this crew which attacked a U-Boat on 3rd May, 1943.                     *SQUADRON LEADER KEN FIELD*

**Under the African sun...** Flying Officer Weskett and crew of Blackburn built Mark III EK589 'The Kiddy' soon after arrival in Nigeria, destination 270 Squadron at Apapa, January, 1944. EK589 used the individual identity letter V with the Squadron and was Struck Off Charge in July, 1945. Front row (left to right): Sergeant Wood, Flight Lieutenant Martin, Flying Officer Weskett, Flight Sergeant Karren, Flight Sergeant Mennal. Back row (left to right): Flight Sergeant Coate, Sergeant Pickles, Warrant Officer Searle, Flight Sergeant Mack, Flight Sergeant Railton.

*EDDIE RAILTON*

**Home base Northern Ireland...** A well-known aerial view of part of the large flying-boat station on Lough Erne. Originally published in the *Belfast Telegraph* soon after the war ended, this photograph shows 12 Sunderlands and two Catalinas up for maintenance. Opened as RAF Castle Archdale in February, 1941, it changed its name to RAF Lough Erne within days following an Air Ministry decree. The original name was re-instated in January, 1943, and Castle Archdale flew operational patrols throughout four years of the war. This station was long-term home to 201 Squadron, RAF, and the two Canadian Sunderland Squadrons, particularly 423 which spent three years in Northern Ireland. Several other Squadrons were based here for short periods.                     *LEN FISHER/RAF MUSEUM P17741*

**Aussie bound...**Sunderland Mark IIIs ML730, ML731 and ML732 on the water at Rochester in October, 1943, prior to the long journey to Australia. There they joined the RAAF Flying-Boat Transport Flight with the RAAF serials A26-1, A26-2 and A26-3.
*SHORT BROTHERS H1674G*

**Precarious perch...**Flight Sergeant Gerry 'Paddy' Watson (in helmet) and Sergeant Peach defy the laws of gravity on a 461 Squadron Sunderland at Pembroke Dock, 1943.
*SQUADRON LEADER KEN FIELD*

**Home base Wales...**RAF Pembroke Dock in May, 1943, at the beginning of the station's most hectic wartime period. The two pre-war hangers have been superbly camouflaged to blend in with the surroundings but the white-hulled Sunderlands are plain to spot. 'PD', as it was known to all involved with flying-boats, was an RAF Station from 1930 until 1959 and operated Sunderlands for 19 of those years, up until 1957. *GROUP CAPTAIN A M CAREY*

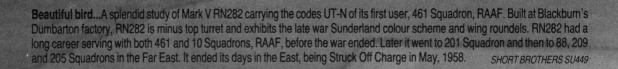

**Beautiful bird...**A splendid study of Mark V RN282 carrying the codes UT-N of its first user, 461 Squadron, RAAF. Built at Blackburn's Dumbarton factory, RN282 is minus top turret and exhibits the late war Sunderland colour scheme and wing roundels. RN282 had a long career serving with both 461 and 10 Squadrons, RAAF, before the war ended. Later it went to 201 Squadron and then to 88, 209 and 205 Squadrons in the Far East. It ended its days in the East, being Struck Off Charge in May, 1958. *SHORT BROTHERS SU449*

**Horse power...**in more ways than one! In front, one mower of two horse power; behind, one Sunderland Mark III of 4,120 horse power! A rural scene at Pembroke Dock belieing the station's wartime role. This particular Sunderland, W4107, served with 228 Squadron before transfer to 302 FTU. While on a ferry flight overseas in October, 1944, the starboard outer propeller flew off, a not uncommon experience on overworked Pegasus engines. W4107 was Struck Off Charge in January, 1945.

*GROUP CAPTAIN A M CAREY*

**In sheep's clothing**...Sunderland Mark III ML728 was allocated off the Rochester line in September, 1943, to the British Overseas Airways Corporation, adopting the civil registration G-AGIA. India Alpha was one of 24 Mark IIIs delivered new to the airline between January, 1943, and August, 1944. They were first used on the Poole-Lagos route, switching to a new Poole-Cairo service which was inaugurated by G-AGIA in October, 1943. Until early 1946, BOAC operated its Sunderland transports in RAF camouflage and markings with the registration underlined in national colours.

*AVIATION PHOTO NEWS*

**Death throes...**Two photographs of Mark I L5807 ablaze at Kalafrana, Malta, after being attacked at its moorings by German fighters, 27th April, 1941. L5807 was one of 228 Squadron's aircraft involved in the evacuation of Greece. It carried the codes DQ-R and later DQ-F.

*LEN FISHER*

**Out to graze...** but not for long. ML797/P and DP198/W, smart but service weary, in honourable retirement at Seletar, Singapore. There was to be no reprieve from the scrapman for these historic aircraft despite hopes to preserve one and bring it back to the UK. ML797 was earmarked for preservation and prepared for the long flight home. The lack of flying-boat bases on the route led to a change of plan and ML797 - like DP198 - went to the Chinese scrapman. Officially, DP198 was Struck Off Charge on 1st June, 1959, just days after its final flight. ML797 went the same way, its paper 'demise' being 30th June . A splendid era in the RAF's long history had well and truly ended.                          *BILL WHITER*

**Elephants' graveyard...** last resting place for Seletar Sunderlands. Stripped of engines and all useful equipment they await the scrapman's attentions and reincarnation probably into items of domestic use. For these unwanted giants the future was as bleak as the skies overhead.                          *BILL WHITER*

**On the panel...** a Signaller of 205 Squadron working his set in a Sunderland Mark V.

*BILL WHITER*

**Grub up!...** Two cooks certainly do not spoil the broth as they work side-by-side in the galley of a 205 Squadron Sunderland.

*BILL WHITER*

**Mirror image...** PP127 on the water at China Bay, Trincomalee, Ceylon. Built as a Mark V at Rochester, L-Love spent its service time in the Far East on the strength of 205 Squadron, principally at Seletar. *BILL WHITER*

**Veteran...** Beneath stormy skies Mark V RN303 refuels at China Bay, Trincomalee, Ceylon, c October 1958. This Blackburn-built veteran gave splendid service both in the UK and the Far East and was one of the last Sunderlands to fly with 205/209 Squadron. Its first unit was 302 Ferry Training Unit and it then flew in the Far East with 230 and 209 Squadrons. Stints with the Flying-Boat Training Squadron and 230 Squadron in the UK were followed by a final return to the East. RN303 survived, at least on paper, until January, 1959, when it was officially Struck Off Charge.

*BILL WHITER*

**Farewell flypast...** ML797 leads the way in the final RAF Sunderland flypast over Singapore, 15th May, 1959. Taken from DP198 which is closely tucked in alongside.                                        *BILL WHITER*

**Waterborne no more...** DP 198 after beaching at Seletar, Singapore, probably following its last flight in May, 1959. One of the 35 Sunderlands built at the Short's Windermere factory, it began life as a Mark III and served witth 423 Squadron, RCAF, before conversion to Mark V status. Far Eastern service with 205 and 209 Squadrons was followed by a return to the UK and to 201 Squadron at Pembroke Dock. DP198, as A-Able, was the last RAF Sunderland to land on the Thames, dropping in for the Battle of Britain Week in September, 1956, with Flight Lieutenant Alan Nicoll as skipper. When 201 Squadron disbanded DP198 headed East again and, eventually, into aviation history.        *BILL WHITER*

**High and dry...** Mark V F-Freddie of 201 Squadron outside one of RAF Pembroke Dock's huge flying-boat hangars. Late on in the Sunderlands' UK service the Pembroke Dock based units adopted the Squadron numbers in front of the roundel, as in 201-F. *JOHN HIRST*

**Taking shape...** A long-term restoration project centres around Mark V ML796 at the Imperial War Museum's Duxford Airfield. This aircraft has had an unusual career, to say the least. Built at Rochester it was the first production Mark V, the final Sunderland variant. It was delivered to Calshot in May, 1945, too late for war service, and soon after joined 228 Squadron at Pembroke Dock, but the Squadron disbanded in June. In 1946 ML796 spent a few months with 4 OTU at Alness before going into storage at Wig Bay, Stranraer. Recalled to service with 230 Squadron for the Berlin Airlift, it was later chosen as one of the 19 Sunderlands to be reconditioned at Belfast for service with the French Navy. ML796 was transferred to the Aeronavale in August, 1951, spending nine years with Flotille 7FE (later 27F) at Dakar, West Africa. Retirement came in December, 1960, and the aircraft went into store in France, having logged 2,400 flying-hours. A new - indeed unique - career began five years later when the much travelled Sunderland was converted into a disco in Northern France, later becoming a nightclub and restaurant, complete with spiral staircase and bar! ML796 came up for disposal in 1976 and was acquired by the Imperial War Museum. In order to transport it to the UK the fuselage had to be cut in half along the horizontal centre line. Housed in Duxford's Superhangar, ML796 is slowly being restored to former glories. It is seen here in May, 1987. *JOHN HILL*

**On the Thames...** In 1982 history was again made when a Sunderland landed on the Thames, the first to do so for nearly a quarter of a century. Sunderland G-BJHS, ex-ML814, was moored by Tower Bridge very close to another veteran, HMS Belfast *JOHN HILL*

**Sandringham...** The centrepoint of the Southampton Hall of Aviation is the magnificently restored Short Sandringham *Beachcomber* which, in 1943, began life as Sunderland Mark III JM715. Built at the Rochester factory, it saw no war service, being held in reserve at RAF Wig Bay, Stranraer. The air frame was one of those chosen for 'civilisation' which included removing all turrets and military equipment, replacing the Pegasus engines with Twin Wasps and partitioning the hull into separate compartments. Now a Sandringham it flew for 33 years in New Zealand, Australia and the West Indies before being rescued from dereliction in Puerto Rico, made airworthy and brought back to the UK in 1980. The Atlantic crossing proved to be its last flight. Subsequently acquired by the Science Museum (London and National Heritage Trust) the Sandringham found a permanent home at the new Southampton Hall of Aviation where today it is resplendent in the colours of Ansett Airways of Australia with its old name of *Beachcomber*. *AUTHOR*

# V. SEEK, STRIKE AND RESCUE

**Headlines...**Fifteen days after war was declared in September, 1939, came a rescue involving Sunderlands which made headline news worldwide. On 18th September the tramp steamer *Kensington Court*, on passage from Argentina to Liverpool with a cargo of wheat, encountered a U-Boat 100 miles south-west of the Bishop Rock. The U-Boat first shelled the 4,863 ton Court Line vessel and then torpedoed it. The ship's SOS was answered by Sunderlands from 228 and 204 Squadrons, two of which - captained by Acting Flight Lieutenants Thurston Smith (228) and John Barrett (204) - landed on the sea and between them took the 34 crewmen aboard. Another 228 aircraft, captained by Squadron Leader Menzies, attacked the U-Boat. The crew of the *Kensington Court* soon found themselves on dry land and this first-ever rescue of seamen by the RAF attracted much publicity. The captains of the two rescuing Sunderlands were each awarded the Distinguished Flying Cross, receiving the medals from the hand of King George VI in November. The photograph shows the *Kensington Court* down by the stern as its lifeboat approaches the 228 Squadron Sunderland. Another flying-boat keeps watch overhead.                                          *GROUP CAPTAIN DAVID BEVAN-JOHN*

**Gongs up...**Proudly wearing their medals - plus the obligatory bags containing gas masks - are the five airmen who attended an investiture by the King in November, 1939. Left to right: Flying Officer Andrew McPhearson, DFC (award made for reconnaissance flights in September); Acting Flight Lieutenant Thurston Smith, DFC (228 Squadron); Acting Squadron Leader Ken Doran, DFC (awarded for an attack on an enemy cruiser); Acting Flight John Barrett, DFC (204 Squadron), and Sergeant W E Willits, DFM. Sergeant Pilot Willits, who served at RAF Pembroke Dock prior to training as a pilot, won the Distinguished Flying Medal for bringing his aircraft home after the pilot had been shot in a combat with an enemy flying-boat, September, 1939.

*TED WILLITS*

**Twixt sea and sky...**The lonely vigil of the Sunderland crews is epitomized by this photograph. Both elements were potential enemies in their own right.          *SQUADRON LEADER KEN FIELD*

**On the receiving end...**A Sunderland's view of a heavily armed German flak ship badly mauled by HMS Mauritius off the Brest Peninsula, 24th August, 1944. Taken by Sunderland H of 228 Squadron. *M N ANDERSON*

**One of many...**A Spanish fishing vessel located by a Sunderland of 422 Squadron, RCAF, at position 49°47'N, 11°23'W. French and Spanish fishing boats were so often seen by the flying-boat crews. At night a 'blip' on the radar screen could be a harmless fishing boat - or a U-Boat bristling with guns. *DR DAVID STEWART*

**Torpedoed!...**A late war casualty was the new American Liberty ship *Jonas Lie,* torpedoed in the Bristol Channel approaches by U-1055 on 9th January, 1945. The 7,176 gross ton vessel, on a voyage from Swansea to New York, was abandoned by its crew after the torpedo hit. Watched by a Pembroke Dock Sunderland, a tug took the striken vessel in tow. Later the tow rope parted and the ship was not found again. It was presumed to have sunk.

*DR DAVID STEWART*

**Last patrol...**Ever vigilant, the crew of ML778, NS-Z of 201 Squadron, keep watch over a convoy during the final official escort patrol of the war, on 3rd/4th June, 1945. Convoys continued to be protected after VE-Day because of fears that some German U-Boats would not surrender. Z-Zebra, up from Castle Archdale, had 201's Commanding Officer, Wing Commander John Barrett, DFC, at the controls. Off the Rochester line as a Mark III, ML778 served with 422 Squadron, RCAF (as 2-S) and 461 Squadron, RAAF, before conversion to Mark V standard. This aircraft had a long post-war career, serving with 201 Squadron and 4 OTU. A new life, and a new language, came in May, 1951, when ML778 transferred to the French Navy. *J L WATSON*

**Eyeball to eyeball...**A so close view of the arch enemy, a German U-Boat. This unidentified U-Boat had the German cross emblazoned on the front of the conning tower.
*CLIFF AUSTIN*

**Straddle!...**Sunderland M of 461 Squadron, piloted by Flight Lieutenant 'Chick' Clarke, depth charging U-106 in the Bay of Biscay, 2nd August, 1943. Clarke and his crew joined forces with Pembroke Dock comrades Flight Lieutenant 'Hank' Hanbury and crew, flying JM708, N of 228 Squadron. Their joint efforts saw the end of a U-Boat which had sunk over 130,000 tons of Allied shipping in 2½ years of prowling the sea lanes.
*DR JOCK ROLLAND/M N ANDERSON*

**The quarry...**U-106, seen from very close in, during the joint action on 2nd August, 1943, involving crews of 228 and 461 Squadrons from Pembroke Dock.
*GROUP CAPTAIN A M CAREY/H THRELFALL*

**Confirmed...** The final journey of U-625 begins as survivors take to the grey Atlantic waters, 10th March, 1944. This U-Boat was sunk by Flight Lieutenant Sid Butler, an RAF pilot serving with 422 Squadron, RCAF. *HARRY THRELFALL*

**Night into day...** Flares dropped by Sunderland ML760, S-Sugar, of 201 Squadron, dramatically reveal a German U-Boat under attack. In the early morning of 7th June, 1944 - D-Day plus one - Flight Lieutenant Les Baveystock, DFC, DFM, and crew caught U-955 on the surface off Gijon, Spain. The depth charge attack was lethal and U-955 went to the bottom. For this action Les Baveystock won a Bar to his DFC, adding a DSO in August when - flying EJ150 - he accounted for U-107. *M N ANDERSON*

**Surrender...** The black flag flying above the conning tower indicates that this German U-Boat is surrendering to the watchful Sunderland above, a scene often repeated in May, 1945. This and the other flags of surrender signified that, at long last, the unremitting war against the U-Boat which had lasted five years and eight months was finally over. *DR DAVID STEWART*

**Into history...**Looking for all the world like a stranded whale, Sunderland Mark II, T9114, of 461 Squadron, RAAF, lies high and dry on Angle Airfield, near Pembroke Dock, May, 1943. On the 29th of the month Flying Officer Gordon Singleton and crew wrote themselves into aviation history by landing the flying-boat on the airfield after a 7 ft hole had been stove in the hull during a dramatic take-off at sea. The Australians had landed in the open sea to rescue survivors from crashed Whitley and Sunderland aircraft, and had to remain waterborne. After transferring the survivors and some of the crew to a naval vessel - and after being towed in heavy seas - Singleton opted to take off, this being accomplished at the cost of a ruptured hull. The historic landing, on the grass alongside a runway, was a remarkable feat and the aircraft suffered little further damage. T9114, one of the first of the Blackburn-built Sunderlands, was recovered from the airfield. Six hedges were removed to bring the aircraft to a beach but T9114 never returned to the water. It was unceremoniously scrapped on the beach - a sad end for a history-making aircraft. Today, Gordon Singleton's remarkable landing is remembered on a plaque at West Angle Bay. This was unveiled in 1992 to commemorate the part played by the Angle airfield in wartime.

*AUSTRALIAN WAR MEMORIAL 128213*

# AVISO

EL día 20 de abril el Almirantazgo británico avisó oficial-mente por radio que las embarcaciones pesqueras que penetrasen en las zonas declaradas peligrosas para la navegación comercial, lo harían por su propia cuenta y riesgo.

Aunque los pesqueros españoles han hecho caso omiso de este aviso, los aviadores ingleses, por consideración hacia los súbditos de un país neutral, no atacaron esos barcos españoles aunque la ley de guerra les autoriza plenamente para hacerlo.

Las fuerzas aéreas de las Naciones Unidas no pueden mantener más tiempo su actitud pasiva, ni permitir nuevas infracciones.

Hoy os damos un último aviso. A partir del día 1 de junio toda embarcación española hallada en zona prohibida será tratada como enemiga y atacada al momento sin previo aviso.

# MARINS PECHEURS FRANÇAIS

Malgré les avertissements successifs que l'Amirauté britannique vous a transmis, vous avez repris votre pêche en haute mer.

Votre présence gêne notre offensive contre les sous-marins.

Vous n'avez maintenant que trois possibilités :

1. Rentrer immédiatement dans vos ports et y rester ;

ou

2. Rallier immédiatement un port britannique ;

ou bien

3. Poursuivre votre pêche et devenir l'objet de nos attaques.

Les avions de la R.A.F., chargés de patrouiller les zones interdites aux bateaux de pêche, ont reçu l'ordre de tirer sur tout bateau qui n'est pas visiblement en train de rentrer à son port d'attache ou de gagner la côte anglaise.

Faites circuler d'urgence ce mot d'ordre parmi vos camarades rencontrés en mer et à tous les équipages à terre.

**Words of warning...**It wasn't only depth charges that the Sunderland crews were called upon to drop. These are examples of warning leaflets in French and Spanish which were dropped upon fishing vessels of both nations.

*ALAN LACY*

# VI. AGAINST THE RISING SUN

**On the way home...**A final photograph for the men of 230 Squadron as they prepare to depart from Seletar, Singapore, for home waters, April 1946. Nearly 280 men drape themselves in, on and around a Mark V Sunderland, joining the Commanding Officer, Wing Commander D E Hawkins, DFC, for this historic shot. The longest serving of all the Sunderland squadrons, 230 had an eventful war, flying in various overseas theatres as the tide of conflict fluctuated. The squadron made a major contribution to the war in the Mediterranean in 1940-43, its Sunderlands participating in the evacuations of Greece and Crete as well as sinking several Italian submarines. A move to the East came in 1944, and with it a multitude of roles including flying in supplies to Chindits operating behind the Japanese lines. In April, 1946, came a return to the UK for the first time in 10 years, and when 230 finally disbanded as a flying-boat unit in 1957 it had operated the mighty Sunderland for an unequalled 19 years. *JIM BRISLEY/D RICHINGS*

**Back to Seletar...**In November, 1945, 230 Squadron returned to its pre-war station of Seletar, Singapore, latterly occupied by the men of the Rising Sun.This was the scene soon after the Squadron's arrival,with two Sunderlands beached between the hangers. *D RICHINGS*

**Men of 230...** Taking a welcome break from working on Sunderlands in the Seletar sun. In the background is Mark V RN304, S-Sugar, which was to have long associations with 230 Squadron and later with the Flying-Boat Training Squadron in the UK. RN304, built by Blackburns, survived until 1957, being Struck Off Charge in the September.                    *JIM BRISLEY*

**Two-six, heave...** Back straining work as 230 manpower is called up to steady a Sunderland as it is eased down the slipway towards the water, probably at Seletar.                    *D RICHINGS*

**Typically tropical...**PP107/W, a Mark V off the Rochester line, beached among the palm trees at Koggala, Ceylon. One of 230 Squadron's aircraft it carries a repeat of the serial number of the fin - an unusual variation. PP107 stayed on in the Far East with 209 and 205 Squadrons and was tragically lost on 28th January, 1951, when it flew into Mount Morrison, Taiwan. *RAF MUSEUM P18804*

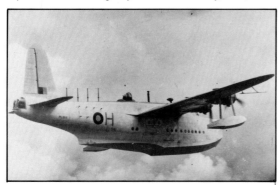

**SEAC bird...**The faired main step of the Mark III Sunderland is shown to advantage in this shot of ML868/H, one of 230 Squadron's 'boats. ML868, a Blackburn product, carries South East Asia Command roundel and fin flash, plus a full array of ASV aerials. After its war service ML868 was Struck Off Charge in January, 1946. *RAF MUSEUM P2003*

**Three up...**A formation of Mark IIIs of 270 Squadron - an unusual sight in wartime. Nearest is DW109/Q with ML867/N and an unidentified third - code letter B - in close attendance. Based at Apapa, Nigeria, 270 Squadron flew Sunderlands from December, 1943, until disbandment in June, 1945, performing necessary if mundane roles in a far off theatre away from much of the action. Of these Sunderlands, DW109, built at Belfast, went to the scrapman in 1947 while ML867 was Struck Off Charge in June, 1945, when the Squadron disbanded. Both N and B have unusual, oversized code letters. *RAF MUSEUM P20755*

# VII. IN PEACEFUL SKIES

**On the Airlift...**PP117, carrying the 4X codes of 230 Squadron, photographed when taking part in the Berlin Airlift. Sunderlands of 230 and its sister squadron, 201, were called up in July, 1948, for Airlift duties. Operating between Finkenwerder on the River Elbe and the Havel See in West Berlin, the flying-boats performed splendidly, carrying 4¹/ tons of supplies into the beleaguered city on each trip. The 'cargo' on the return was a mixture of manufactured goods and refugees. In a slick operation, lasting six months, the Sunderlands made over 1,000 sorties, carrying 4,500 tons of food and airlifting out some 1,100 German youngsters. Salt was carried in large quantities by the Sunderlands which were uniquely able to cope with such corrosive material. The flying-boat part of the Airlift ended just before Christmas when the Havel See began to ice up.                                                                    *ALEX DONALDSON*

**Lined up...**A photograph which once graced the office of the Station Commander of RAF Pembroke Dock - four Mark Vs of 201 Squadron in close formation in the 1950s. Nearest is SZ576, A-Able, which after RAF service went to the French Navy in July, 1957.

*H HALL VIA P MORFEE*

**Hull down...** ML817 displaying for the crowds at RAF Biggin Hill's Battle of Britain Day, September, 1953. It had an eventful service life, progressively with MAEE, 201, 423 (RCAF), 330 (Norwegian) and 230 Squadrons as well as a stint with 235 OCU. It was Struck Off Charge in October, 1957. *PETER CLIFTON*

**Waterline...** C-Charlie, PP115, of 201 Squadron, seen some time before April, 1951, when the wartime code combinations - in this case NS - were abandoned. Judging by the distinct waterline around the hull this Sunderland had spent a long time afloat. PP115 served in wartime with 461 and 10 Squadrons, RAAF, and in peacetime with 201 and 230 Squadrons. It was Struck Off Charge on 30th July, 1955. *JEFF LLOYD*

**Home base Calshot...** The story of the RAF and its flying-boats is richly intertwined with Calshot, Hampshire, a 'mecca' for marine aviation in Britain from before the First World War. Built on a strip of land jutting out into the Solent, it took its name from Calshot Castle, the ancient fortification located on the Spit. A training and first line station before World War II, it was not used operationally during the war but fulfilled many and varied roles connected with flying-boats and marine craft. With the return of peace, 201 and 230 Squadrons brought their Sunderlands to Calshot in 1946, remaining until early 1949. No 4 OTU moved in from Alness in 1947, changing its title to 235 OCU. Sunderlands finally left the station in October, 1953, and the RAF Ensign was lowered for the last time in May, 1961. This photograph was taken in the very early 1950s. *FRANK DENYER*

**Trainer...**PP130, of 235 Operational Conversion Unit, up from Calshot in the early 1950s, tasked with training new Sunderland crews. This aircraft was Struck Off Charge in June, 1955.                    *SQUADRON LEADER BILL HOLLOWAY*

**Wing walkers...**The airmen on the starboard wing of PP117, A-W of 201 Squadron, were certainly not there to have a suntan! When taxiing out during a detachment at Castle Archdale in the mid 1950s, PP117 hit an obstruction which wiped off the port float. A scramble onto the opposite wingtip by several of the crew saved the day until a marine craft came alongside to lend support. PP117 lived to fly another day, finally being Struck Off Charge in October, 1957.                    *ERIC ROBERTS*

**Casualty...**NJ267, B-Baker of 201 Squadron, broken and disfigured near Pembroke Dock after crashing on take off in March, 1954. This was Pembroke Dock's worst post-war flying-boat accident and cost the lives of seven men. The heroism of Flight Sergeant Ernest 'Darky' Evans, the Sunderland's Engineer, who twice went back into the waterlogged aircraft to rescue crewmates, was later recognised by the award of the George Medal.                                                                   *JOHN BECKETT*

**Home base Pembroke Dock...** The last operational flying-boat station in the UK was Pembroke Dock which finally said farewell to its squadrons in early 1957. For much of the post-war years Pembroke Dock had been home to both 201 and 230 Squadrons, later augmented by the Flying-Boat Training Squadron. Pembroke Dock was always a happy station. A posting to the wilds of West Wales may at first have seemed like the end of the earth - within a matter of days Pembroke Dock became a home from home. This aerial view was taken in April, 1956 - just months before the Sunderlands said their final farewells.                               *GERRY MORBEY*

**Down at Gib...**Z-Zebra, SZ567 of 230 Squadron, seen on the water at Gibraltar, December, 1956, shows the revised codings adopted in the UK at the end of the flying-boat era. Two months later 230 Squadron disbanded and this Belfast built veteran was pensioned off, being Struck Off Charge in October, 1957.

*SQUADRON LEADER BILL HOLLOWAY/JOHN HIRST*

**For the scrapman...**Sunderland V NJ180, masquerading under the ground instructional airframe number of 7146M, being scrapped at Pembroke Dock in 1954. This aircraft is believed to have been damaged at its moorings during a gale. Built by Blackburns as a Mark III, NJ180 first served with the Norwegians of 330 Squadron. After conversion to Mark V standard it was on charge with the Flying-Boat Training Squadron. *ERIC ROBERTS*

**NCOs all...**Flight Sergeant 'Shep' Shepherd and his 201 Squadron crew at Pembroke Dock c April, 1954. They are thought to be the last all NCO crew to operate in Sunderlands. Back row (left to right): --------; Sergeant Pete Rich (Signaller); Flight Sergeant 'Darky' Evans, GM (Engineer); -----. Front row (left to right): Sergeant Bill Whiter (Navigator); Sergeant Warren (Co-Pilot); Flight Sergeant Shepherd (Captain) and Flight Sergeant Tennant (Navigator). *BILL WHITER*

**Arctic airlift...**Squadron Leader Jim Higgins, DFC, AFC, Commanding Officer of 230 Squadron, and his crew about to board Sunderland O-Oboe at Pembroke Dock in July, 1952 - destination Greenland. The Pembroke Dock based Sunderlands of 230 and 201 Squadrons provided vital support for the British North Greenland Expedition, flying in supplies over nearly 200 miles from Young Sound on the eastern side of Greenland to Britannia Lake, the Expedition's base camp. Oboe was the 'pathfinder' of the five 230 Squadron aircraft which in 1952 ferried in 150 tons of supplies to the Lake. Joining Squadron Leader Higgins and crew was the Expedition Leader, Commander C J Wilson, RN. In 1953 the supply tasks were undertaken by 201 Squadron and in 1954, 230 Squadron had the satisfaction of ferrying home the Expedition members, plus their huskies, landing at Pembroke Dock.

*BILL WING*

**Tale of a tail...**Two airmen hard at work on maintenance at Young Sound - or could it be that they are doing a spot of fishing? All part of the support of the British North Greenland Expedition.

*BILL WING*

**Dog meets Dog...**'Joanna', one of the dozen huskies flown from Greenland to the UK in August, 1954, makes friends with Flight Lieutenant Don Wynne, a 230 Squadron pilot, and his Navigator. Appropriately, Don Wynne was flying D-Dog, VB889, borrowed from 201 Squadron for the Arctic trip and the photograph was taken before the aircraft left Greenland. Four 230 Squadron aircraft airlifted 21 members of the British North Greenland Expedition to Pembroke Dock where they received a tumultuous welcome. The huskies - after a period in quarantine - were shipped out to the Falkland Islands, the other end of the earth from their earlier 'home'. An offspring of one of the huskies was retained by 230 Squadron as a mascot. It was called 'Kita'. *BILL WING*

**FBTS men...**The officers and instructors of the Flying-Boat Training Squadron pose for an official photograph at RAF Pembroke Dock, c 1955. Perhaps a better choice of background scenery could have been made although R S Hayes Ltd, the Pembroke Dock based shipbuilders and engineers, would have been the last to complain!
*GERRY MORBEY*

**Trophies galore...**Even in the autumn of its service life the Sunderland was still a potent and competitive aircraft, as can be judged by all the silverware collected by 201 Squadron at Pembroke Dock. The trophies get pride of place as the officers and men of 201 join with the CO, Squadron Leader D G Baird, for this official photograph taken in the early part of 1956. In August of the previous year 201 was awarded the Aird-Whyte Trophy for weapons efficiency in RAF Coastal Command squadrons. Another Aird-Whyte trophy - for swimming efficiency - came the squadron's way in the November. In May, 1956, came the announcement that 201 had won the Coastal Command inter-squadron trophy, pipping its sister unit, 230, for the silverware. Icing on the cake came in the same month when it was revealed that the Dunning Memorial Cup for 1955 - awarded to the squadron achieving the highest standard during the year at the joint anti-submarine school - had also come to 201. RAF Pembroke Dock became, in 1955, the first RAF unit to win the Brackley Memorial Trophy for outstanding work in flying-boats. Awarded by the Guild of Air Pilots and Air Navigators it was made in recognition of the part played by 201 and 230 Squadrons in the Greenland Expedition, 1951-54.
*BILL WHITER*

**Every inch a lady...**PP154 of 205 Squadron in one of its natural elements, photographed by Master Engineer V M Reeve in 1952. One of a batch of Mark Vs built at Blackburn's Dumbarton factory, PP154 was too late to see war sevice but joined 230 Squadron at Seletar in 1946, being coded Y-Yoke. Lengthy storage in the UK was followed by allocation to 205 Squadron, Singapore, using the letters X and then N. Transferred to 209 Squadron in January, 1953, it returned to the UK the following year, only to languish at the Flying-Boat Servicing Unit at Wig Bay until being sold as scrap in September, 1957 - going the same way as all but a mere handful of its famous sisters.                                    *V M REEVE*

**Beached...**ML881, X-Xray of 209 Squadron, on beaching gear outside a Seletar hanger, c 1950-51. It carries the name Rajang River. Built by Blackburns as a Mark III, ML881 served with 201 Squadron (as NS-P) before conversion to a Mark V. While moored at Castle Archdale in March, 1945, it was struck by a tender but was repaired. ML881 ended its days with 209 Squadron, being Struck Off Charge in September, 1957.     *ERIC ROBERTS*

**New boys...** The only new Sunderland squadron to form after the end of the war was No 88. It was born on 1st September, 1946, out of 1430 Flight at Kai Tak, Hong Kong, and was tasked initially with transport duties, providing courier services between Far Eastern bases. Later the squadron was re-designated a general reconnaissance unit, flying shipping and anti-piracy patrols. Sunderlands again went to war in June, 1950, when the Korean conflict broke out. Flying from Iwakuni, 88 Squadron patrolled the Korean coastline for a year before being withdrawn to Seletar. Later it again took up a warlike role, flying 165 missions against Malayian terrorists before disbanding in October, 1954. This photograph was taken at Kai Tak in 88 Squadron's early days as a Sunderland unit - probably between 1946 and 1948. In the centre of the group is the Commanding Officer, Squadron Leader Duggie Gall. *GERRY MORBEY*

**History makers...**Flight Lieutenant Ken Letford, DSO, DFC, and five crew members of the Yangtse Incident Sunderland, ML772, pose for a crew shot some time before the April, 1949, missions to HMS Amethyst. Back row (left to right): Gerry Morbey; Don Gray (Signals Leader, 88 Squadron, who was not on the Yangtse flights); 'Lofty' Doyle; ---- Price. Front row (left to right): Maurice Marshall; Ken Letford and Ken Dillon. *GERRY MORBEY*

**Last of the line...**A misty, moody shot of SZ599, the last of the 749 Sunderlands built at four locations - Rochester, Windermere, Belfast and Dumbarton. SZ599 came off the Short and Harland line at Belfast on 14th June, 1946, and spent a lengthy time with MAEE at Felixstowe. Between 1948 and 1950 it was involved in main step experiments, being given a fully faired main step with natural ventilation of the afterbody. Following its Felixstowe days SZ599 became a run-of-the-mill squadron aircraft in the Far East with 88, 205 (as Y) and 209 Squadrons. It did not survive to witness the end of the fine Sunderland era, being Struck Off Charge on 21st June, 1954. *SHORT BROTHERS AC5 1249*

**Home base Kai Tak...**Four Sunderlands lie at anchor off RAF Station Kai Tak, Hong Kong, in the late 1940s, while a fifth is beached within the station. Kai Tak was home to 88 Squadron for a period. Where the Sunderlands once moored up airliners today land along the much enlarged runway servicing Hong Kong. *GERRY MORBEY*

**From the Yangtse...** Sunderland V ML772, pictured approaching Hong Kong, had, in April 1949, written an RAF chapter into a very naval story - the extraordinary and dangerous events surrounding *HMS Amethyst* trapped by Chinese Communists on the Yangtse River. Piloted by Flight Lieutenant Ken Letford, DSO, DFC, ML772 - D-Dog of 88 Squadron - had been called up to take doctors and medical supplies to the *Amethyst*. On the morning of 21st April Letford and crew, with the station CO of RAF Kai Tak, Group Captain J M Jefferson, two service doctors and two soldiers trained in dropping supplies, left Kai Tak for the Yangtse only to be diverted to Lung Wha, Shanghai, as the frigate was under fire. Later that day the Sunderland landed near the frigate only to be the target of heavy machine-gun fire. The Sunderland was forced to make a hurried take-off, leaving behind just one doctor, Flight Lieutenant Michael Fearnley, RAF. On the following day Letford and ML772 - with a Navy chaplain and replacements for the ship's crew aboard - tried again. They landed alongside but the Communists again fired upon the Sunderland, forcing it to take off immediately. Still operating from Shanghai, ML772 made a reconnaissance of the Yangtse on 23rd April but ground fire forced an early return as the port main fuel tank had been holed. The damaged ML772 was returned to Kai Tak on 24th April by Flying Officer Dick Dulieu who had flown a second Sunderland, NJ176, to Shanghai. No further trips were made to the *Amethyst* and Letford and crew came back to base on 25th April in NJ176. Letford won the Bar to his wartime Bomber Command DFC for this operation and his Yangtse crew was: Flying Officer Maurice Marshall (Navigator); Pilot II Ken Dillon (Second Pilot); Engineer I 'Lofty' Doyle; Signaller I Gerry Morbey; Signaller II Price; Gunner II Devany, along with Group Captain Jefferson.

As for ML772, it had begun life as a Rochester built Mark III. It had two accidents at Castle Archdale in 1945 when with 201 Squadron (as S-Sugar) and conversion to Mark V standard followed. An historic aircraft because of its part in the Yangtse incident, ML772 could have been a candidate for preservation. Sadly, this was not to be and ML772 was discarded by the RAF in 1955 - its Struck Off Charge being 30th June.

*GERRY MORBEY.*

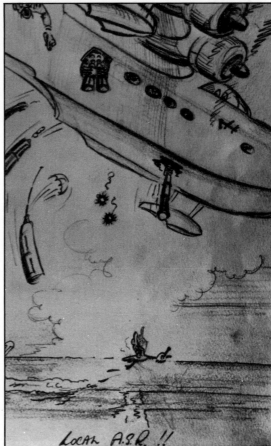

**Seagull ahoy!**...A cartoon inspired by an air-sea rescue mission carried out by 230 Squadron off the Welsh coast in the 1950s. Looking for an aircraft reported to have crashed off St. Davids, the Sunderland homed in by radar onto a lone Seagull which was just disturbing the surface of the calm sea!

*BILL WING*

**Slipway Charlie...**A once so familiar sight at flying-boat stations all over the world - a Sunderland on its beaching gear at the end of a slipway. In this case it is DP199/C of 88 Squadron in the Far East, taken some time before June, 1951, when this aircraft was Struck Off Charge. Windermere built, DP199 served as a Mark III with 461 Squadron, RAAF, before it was uprated to Mark V standard.
*GERRY MORBEY*

**Last sortie...**Flight Lieutenant Ben Ford, a long time Sunderland man, and his crew who flew the last operational sortie in an RAF Sunderland, 14th May, 1959. The aircraft was DP 198/W of 205/209 Squadron and the sortie was with HMS Caprice. In the photograph are (left to right): Master Engineer Dickie Knott; Master Signaller Bill Williams; Flight Sergeant Jock Armitage (Signaller); Flight Sergeant Ted Bevis (Signaller); Flight Sergeant 'Butch' Tait (Navigator); Flight Lieutenant Ben Ford (Captain); Wing Commander R A N Macready (O C 205/209 Squadron); Flight Lieutenant Jack Poyser (Co-pilot); Flight Lieutenant Joe Josey (Signaller); Master Signaller 'Rocky' Rochford and Flight Sergeant Bill Whiter (Navigator).
*BILL WHITER*

**In best K D...**Sunderland NJ193 towers impressively over the officers and men of 205 Squadron as they line up for a squadron photograph at Seletar, c 1955. A Far Eastern Squadron from as far back as 1929, 205 flew Sunderlands from June, 1945, until May, 1959, being the last operational flying-boat squadron in the RAF. For the last 2$^1/_2$ years of its existence the Squadron was known as 205/209 Squadron, reflecting the link-up in January, 1955, when 209 was disbanded into its sister. Blackburn built Sunderland NJ193 had a long career, serving with 461 and 10 Squadrons, RAAF, and 201 and 205 Squadrons, RAF. It went to the scrapman in February, 1957.
*DAVE STRUDWICK*

**Compass check...**A navigator checks the master compass on a Sunderland Mark V - a long 'trek' from his table up front.
*JEFF LLOYD*

**Springbok...**As the war came to an end South Africa took delivery of several surplus Sunderlands and these flew with 35 Squadron, South African Air Force, based at Congella, Durban, Natal. This unit adopted RB as its RAF-style code letters - the same combination had once been used with distinction by 10 Squadron, RAAF. Sunderland RB-H - thought to be serial number 1703 - came on a goodwill trip to the UK and is seen beached at RAF Pembroke Dock.
*COLONEL IAN BERGH, SAAF*

**Final flight...**The Royal New Zealand Air Force, which operated 16 Mark Vs in the 1950s and 1960s, was the last military user of the Sunderland. NZ4107/D made history on 2nd April, 1967, when Flight Lieutenant John Laing flew this Sunderland from Lauthala Bay, Fiji, to Hobsonville, Auckland, ending the RNZAF's association with the most famous of all the flying boats. Four months later NZ4107 was broken up at Hobsonville. It had begun life as VB883, one of the last Blackburn batch of 10 Sunderlands, and had served with 302 FTU and 88 Squadron in the RAF.
*VIA MAP*

# VIII. FINALE

**Prototypes...**Air and water studies of the two prototype Mark IVs - subsequently re-named Seafords. In the air is MZ269, showing to good effect the revised shape of the fin and tailplane. Moored up is MZ271, the rakish lines of the Hercules engines further divorcing it from its famous sister. *SHORT BROTHERS H2255H AND RAF MUSEUM P5837*

**Stillborn...**The Short Shetland was planned as the successor to the Sunderland and two of these massive flying-boats were built at Rochester. Conceived in 1940, the Shetland was the result of co-operation in design and manufacture between Short Brothers and Saunders-Roe, both famous names in flying-boat history. It dimensions and performance were impressive - wingspan 150 ft; length 110 ft; all up weight 125,000 lb; maximum speed 263 mph; range 4,000 miles. The first prototype, DX166, was not launched until October, 1944, and made its first flight on 14th December with John Parker at the controls. DX166 - photographed at Rochester in November, 1944 - went to MAEE, Felixstowe, in October, 1945, for service trials and it was here that it was to end its short career in dramatic fashion. On 28th January, 1946, the Shetland was burnt out at its moorings when a generator overheated. The second Shetland - flown in 1947 as a civil transport - survived until 1951 when it was scrapped.     *AVIATION PHOTO NEWS*

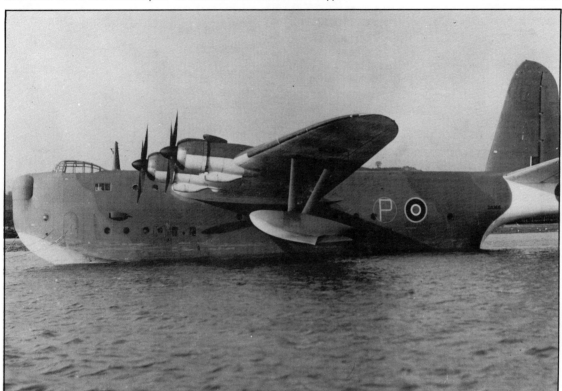

**Mark Four...**In its original form, Sunderland Mark IV prototype MZ269 sits perched on a Rochester slipway in May, 1944, three months before its first flight. Powered by 1,700 hp Bristol Hercules engines driving four-bladed propellors, the Mark IV initially had a standard fin and rudder and the original small dihedral tailplane. First flown on 30th August, various problems were encountered, resulting in an enlarged fin with a forward dorsal extension and a larger tailplane being fitted - radically changing the Sunderland look. Two Mark IV prototypes - MZ269 and MZ271 - were built and both went to the MAEE at Felixstowe in 1945. They were used for various trials and general experimental duties before being scrapped in July, 1947, their demise hastened by an engine fire in MZ269. In performance terms the Mark IV was only marginally better than the Sunderland V already in service. A production order for 40 of the new mark - now renamed Seaford - was cut to just eight, and all were converted to civilian Solents.     *SHORT BROTHERS H1923*

# IX. PRESERVATION

**Homecoming...**An old warrior comes home to rest as ML824, latterly of the French Navy, makes its last flight on 24th March, 1961, destination Pembroke Dock. Fittingly, the escort of two Shackletons was provided by 201 Squadron, RAF - the unit which in its flying-boat years once operated ML824 as Z-Zebra. ML824, built at Belfast, had been transferred to the Aeronavale in October, 1951, after wartime service with 201 and 330 (Norwegian) Squadrons and a lengthy period in storage. The French operated their Sunderlands at Dakar, West Africa, until the last three were withdrawn from service in 1960. ML824 was presented by the French Government to the Sunderland Trust for preservation at Pembroke Dock, and it was to remain on display just inside the old Dockyard wall for a decade. Prime mover behind the Sunderland Trust was a then West Wales farmer, Peter Thomas, whose foresight, initiative and perseverance saw not only the saving of at least one example of the Sunderland but led ultimately to the establishment of a healthy aircraft preservation movement in the UK. He later set up Britain's first aircraft museum - Skyfame - at Staverton Airport, Gloucester. *VIA TONY WILLIAMS*

**Weatherworn...**Showing the effects of 10 years on display in the salt laden elements of Pembroke Dock, ML824 faces up to a new future in the Spring of 1971. The Sunderland was dismantled into manageable sections and transported to London and to the new RAF Museum at Hendon. The wings and tailplane went by road; the hull was transported by sea in an Army landing craft. Discussing the task in hand are men of No 71 Maintenance Unit, RAF Bicester. Even by their standards, the Sunderland presented a major task.

**Indignity!...**What a way to treat a lady! After being brought up the Thames ML824 suffers the indignity of being strapped on to a low loader for the journey to Hendon Museum. There - after several years in store - the Sunderland was restored and placed on display, initially outside and then in the Battle of Britain hanger. Today it wears the 1945 code combination of NS-Z from its wartime days with 201 Squadron. Z-Zebra is a fine memorial not only to a splendid aircraft type but to a whole era of aviation which sadly has gone forever. *VIA RAF ABINGDON*

**The office...**The much changed pilots' panel of G-BJHS as seen when the Sunderland was moored on the Thames in 1982.
*AUTHOR*

**Lovely lines...**The world's last flying example of the Sunderland made history in 1982 by landing on the Thames, and is seen moored in the shadow of London's Tower Bridge. Registered G-BJHS, it was then owned by Edward Hulton and had returned to the UK in March, 1981, after a remarkable and varied career. Built as a Mark III by Short and Harland at Belfast, its first identity was the RAF serial number ML814, and it went to war with both 201 RAF and 422 RCAF Squadrons prior to conversion to a Mark V. It then operated with 330 (Norwegian) Squadron, RAF, before being 'mothballed' at Wig Bay. Rescued by the Royal New Zealand Air Force, it was refurbished at Belfast and became NZ4108 in June, 1953, flying over 1,000 hours with the RNZAF before again going into storage. In 1963, NZ4108 was sold to Airlines of New South Wales and took up the Australian civil registration VH-BRF. It was not returned to Short Brothers for conversion to Sandringham standard; instead this work was carried out in Australia, resulting in a blunter nose profile than the Sandringhams. In Australian service called *Islander*, it took on a new identity when acquired by Captain Charles Blair of Antilles Air Boats. It went to the Virgin Islands and was allocated the US registration N158J. Brought home from the Virgin Islands by Edward Hulton, G-BJHS spent most of the next dozen years in the UK, latterly at Calshot. In 1993 this venerable lady was acquired by American collector Kermit Weeks who -with regular pilot Ken Emmott - flew the Sunderland across the Atlantic to the United States. Its new home is in the sunshine state of Florida where it remains in flying condition. *AUTHOR*

**Queenie...**NZ4115, Q-Queenie when in service in 1962 with the RNZAF's 5 Squadron. After being in reserve this Sunderland was allocated for preservation to the Museum of Transport and Technology at Auckland. It is the former RAF SZ584.                    *MAP*

**Relic...**All that is sadly left of NZ4112, once one of the 16 Mark Vs operated by the Royal New Zealand Air Force. NZ4112 - formerly Dumbarton built VB881 - was sold after retirement and presented to the Hobsonville Yacht Club, Auckland. There was to be no long term future for this venerable lady and the Sunderland was subsequently scrapped. The Ferrymead Aeronautical Society of Christchurch did manage to save the gutted cockpit and nose section, as seen here in 1981.                    *W A C GILMOUR*